EMMANUEL JOSEPH

Cultural Currents, How Social Dynamics and Emotional Intelligence Shape Ethical Innovation

Copyright © 2025 by Emmanuel Joseph

All rights reserved. No part of this publication may be reproduced, stored or transmitted in any form or by any means, electronic, mechanical, photocopying, recording, scanning, or otherwise without written permission from the publisher. It is illegal to copy this book, post it to a website, or distribute it by any other means without permission.

First edition

*This book was professionally typeset on Reedsy.
Find out more at reedsy.com*

Contents

1. Chapter 1: The Tapestry of Culture — 1
2. Chapter 2: The Dance of Social Dynamics — 3
3. Chapter 3: Emotional Intelligence: The Heartbeat of... — 5
4. Chapter 4: The Synergy of Social and Emotional Intelligence — 7
5. Chapter 5: Ethical Frameworks in Innovation — 9
6. Chapter 6: Cultural Sensitivity in Ethical Innovation — 11
7. Chapter 7: The Role of Empathy in Design Thinking — 13
8. Chapter 8: The Power of Collaboration — 15
9. Chapter 9: Leadership in Ethical Innovation — 17
10. Chapter 10: The Ethics of Technology — 19
11. Chapter 11: Balancing Profit and Purpose — 21
12. Chapter 12: Innovation in the Public Sector — 23
13. Chapter 13: The Role of Education in Ethical Innovation — 25
14. Chapter 14: The Impact of Globalization on Innovation — 27
15. Chapter 15: Ethical Considerations in Research and... — 29
16. Chapter 16: The Role of Media in Shaping Ethical Innovation — 31
17. Chapter 17: The Future of Ethical Innovation — 33

1

Chapter 1: The Tapestry of Culture

In the kaleidoscope of humanity, culture serves as the intricate thread weaving together our shared experiences and societal norms. Each community, shaped by history, geography, and collective values, births unique cultural identities that reflect in their customs, traditions, and worldviews. This rich tapestry of culture not only enriches our global landscape but also underlines the complex nature of social dynamics that govern human interactions. As we embark on this journey, we shall explore how these cultural currents influence the ethical landscape of innovation.

At the heart of every culture lies a unique set of beliefs, values, and practices that define its identity. These cultural elements are often passed down through generations, shaping the way individuals perceive the world and interact with one another. For instance, some cultures prioritize collectivism and community well-being, while others emphasize individualism and personal achievement. These differing cultural orientations significantly impact the approach to innovation, as they influence the priorities and ethical considerations that guide the development of new solutions.

Furthermore, culture acts as a lens through which individuals interpret and respond to social dynamics. The way people communicate, collaborate, and resolve conflicts is deeply rooted in their cultural background. This cultural lens can either facilitate or hinder the innovation process, depending on how well it aligns with the goals and values of the innovative endeavor. By understanding and respecting cultural diversity, we can create an inclusive environment that fosters creativity and ethical decision-making.

In addition to shaping individual behavior, culture also plays a crucial role in defining the ethical frameworks that guide innovation. Ethical principles such as fairness, justice, and respect for human dignity are often rooted in cultural values. These principles serve as a moral compass, ensuring that innovative solutions are not only effective but also aligned with the greater good. By integrating cultural sensitivity into the innovation process, we can ensure that our efforts are respectful, inclusive, and ethically sound.

2

Chapter 2: The Dance of Social Dynamics

Social dynamics play a pivotal role in the fabric of our interactions, dictating the ebb and flow of relationships within communities. These dynamics, shaped by power structures, social roles, and communication patterns, create a fertile ground for collaboration, conflict, and ultimately, progress. The delicate balance of social influence and group behavior often determines the trajectory of societal development. By understanding the dance of social dynamics, we can harness its potential to foster an environment conducive to ethical innovation.

At the core of social dynamics lies the concept of power—how it is distributed, exercised, and challenged within a group. Power dynamics influence decision-making processes, often determining who gets to contribute ideas and who gets to implement them. Acknowledging and addressing power imbalances is essential for creating an inclusive space where diverse voices can be heard and valued. This equitable environment nurtures ethical innovation by ensuring that solutions are developed through a collaborative effort that respects everyone's input.

Communication patterns are another crucial aspect of social dynamics. The way individuals convey and interpret information can either facilitate or hinder the flow of ideas. Open, transparent communication fosters trust and encourages the exchange of diverse perspectives, leading to innovative solutions that are both effective and ethical. Conversely, poor communication can result in misunderstandings, conflicts, and ultimately, the stifling of creativity. By promoting healthy communication practices, we can create a fertile ground for ethical innovation to thrive.

Social roles and group behavior also play a significant role in shaping social dynamics. Each individual within a group often assumes specific roles based on their strengths, expertise, and social standing. These roles influence how people interact with one another and contribute to the innovation process. By recognizing and valuing the unique contributions of each member, we can create a collaborative environment that leverages the diverse talents and perspectives within the group. This inclusivity drives ethical innovation by ensuring that solutions are well-rounded and considerate of various viewpoints.

3

Chapter 3: Emotional Intelligence: The Heartbeat of Innovation

Emotional intelligence, the ability to recognize, understand, and manage our own emotions and those of others, serves as the heartbeat of innovation. This essential skill enables individuals to navigate the complexities of human interactions, fostering empathy, collaboration, and ethical decision-making. As we delve into the intricacies of emotional intelligence, we will uncover its profound impact on shaping innovative solutions that are not only groundbreaking but also ethically sound.

Self-awareness, a key component of emotional intelligence, involves understanding our own emotions and how they influence our thoughts and actions. By cultivating self-awareness, we can identify our strengths and areas for growth, enabling us to contribute more effectively to the innovation process. This introspective understanding also helps us manage our emotions, preventing them from clouding our judgment and ensuring that our decisions are rational and ethical.

Empathy, another crucial aspect of emotional intelligence, involves recognizing and understanding the emotions of others. By putting ourselves in others' shoes, we can gain valuable insights into their needs, desires, and pain points. This empathetic approach fosters collaboration and trust, as individuals feel heard and valued. In the context of innovation, empathy enables us to design solutions that are not only effective but also compassionate and respectful of the diverse experiences of users.

Social skills, the final component of emotional intelligence, encompass a range of abilities that facilitate effective communication and collaboration. These skills include active listening, conflict resolution, and the ability to inspire and motivate others. By honing our social skills, we can create a positive and inclusive environment that encourages the free flow of ideas and fosters ethical innovation. This collaborative atmosphere ensures that diverse perspectives are considered, leading to solutions that are both innovative and ethically sound.

4

Chapter 4: The Synergy of Social and Emotional Intelligence

The interplay between social dynamics and emotional intelligence creates a powerful synergy that drives ethical innovation. By cultivating a deep understanding of both individual emotions and group behavior, we can create a harmonious environment where creativity flourishes and ethical considerations take center stage. This chapter will explore how the fusion of these two forces can lead to transformative solutions that address pressing societal challenges while upholding the highest ethical standards.

The first step in harnessing this synergy is recognizing the interconnectedness of social dynamics and emotional intelligence. Social dynamics influence how individuals interact within a group, while emotional intelligence governs how they understand and manage these interactions. By integrating these two elements, we can create a cohesive framework that promotes collaboration, trust, and ethical decision-making.

One way to achieve this integration is through the practice of active listening. Active listening involves fully engaging with the speaker, acknowledging their perspective, and responding thoughtfully. This practice not only fosters effective communication but also builds trust and rapport among group members. By promoting active listening, we can create an environment where individuals feel heard and valued, leading to more inclusive and ethical innovation.

Another key aspect of this synergy is the role of empathy in bridging cultural and social divides. Empathy enables individuals to understand and appreciate diverse perspectives, fostering a sense of connection and mutual respect. By incorporating empathy into the innovation process, we can create solutions that are not only effective but also culturally sensitive and ethically sound. This approach ensures that the needs and values of diverse communities are considered and respected.

Conflict resolution is another critical component of this synergy. Conflicts are inevitable in any group setting, but how they are managed can significantly impact the innovation process. By leveraging emotional intelligence and understanding social dynamics, we can navigate conflicts constructively, turning them into opportunities for growth and learning. This approach fosters a collaborative and respectful environment, ensuring that innovative solutions are developed through a process that upholds ethical principles.

5

Chapter 5: Ethical Frameworks in Innovation

Innovation, while a catalyst for progress, must be guided by ethical frameworks to ensure its positive impact on society. These frameworks, rooted in cultural values and moral principles, provide a compass for navigating the complex landscape of technological advancements and their societal implications. By examining various ethical paradigms, we can identify the principles that should guide our innovative endeavors, ensuring they align with the greater good and respect the diverse fabric of humanity.

One foundational ethical framework is the principle of beneficence, which emphasizes the importance of promoting the well-being of individuals and communities. In the context of innovation, this principle calls for the development of solutions that enhance the quality of life, address pressing societal challenges, and contribute to the common good. By prioritizing beneficence, we can ensure that our innovative efforts are aligned with the goal of creating a better world for all.

Another key ethical principle is justice, which focuses on fairness and equity in the distribution of resources and opportunities. This principle is particularly relevant in the realm of innovation, as it calls for the development of solutions that are accessible and beneficial to all members of society, regardless of their socioeconomic status, race, or gender. By integrating justice into the innovation process, we can create more inclusive and equitable solutions that address the needs of diverse communities.

Respect for autonomy is another essential ethical principle, which emphasizes the importance of honoring individuals' rights to make informed decisions about their own lives. In the context of innovation, this principle calls for transparency, informed consent, and respect for users' privacy and agency. By prioritizing autonomy, we can ensure that our innovative solutions are developed and implemented in a manner that respects individuals' rights and dignity.

Non-maleficence, the principle of "do no harm," is also a critical ethical consideration in innovation. This principle calls for the careful assessment of potential risks and harms associated with new technologies and solutions, ensuring that they do not cause undue harm to individuals or communities. By integrating non-maleficence into the innovation process, we can mitigate potential negative impacts and create solutions that are safe, responsible, and ethically sound.

6

Chapter 6: Cultural Sensitivity in Ethical Innovation

Cultural sensitivity is paramount in the realm of ethical innovation, as it ensures that new solutions are respectful and inclusive of diverse perspectives. By recognizing and valuing the cultural contexts in which innovations are developed and implemented, we can avoid the pitfalls of ethnocentrism and foster a more equitable and just world. This chapter will delve into the importance of cultural sensitivity, offering strategies for integrating it into the innovation process.

At its core, cultural sensitivity involves an awareness and appreciation of cultural diversity, as well as a commitment to understanding and respecting different cultural norms and values. In the context of innovation, this means recognizing that cultural factors can significantly influence the acceptance and effectiveness of new solutions. By taking these factors into account, we can create innovations that are not only effective but also culturally appropriate and respectful.

One strategy for promoting cultural sensitivity is the practice of inclusive design. Inclusive design involves actively engaging with diverse communities throughout the innovation process, from ideation to implementation. By involving individuals from different cultural backgrounds, we can gain valuable insights into their unique needs, preferences, and challenges. This collaborative approach ensures that the resulting solutions are more inclusive, equitable, and responsive to the diverse experiences of users.

Another important aspect of cultural sensitivity is the recognition and mitigation of cultural biases. Cultural biases can manifest in various forms, such as stereotypes, assumptions, and prejudices, and can significantly impact the innovation process. By actively identifying and addressing these biases, we can create a more inclusive and respectful environment that fosters ethical innovation. This involves continuous reflection, education, and open dialogue about cultural differences and their implications.

Cultural sensitivity also calls for a commitment to ethical cross-cultural communication. Effective cross-cultural communication involves not only linguistic competence but also an understanding of cultural nuances, non-verbal cues, and communication styles. By fostering open, respectful, and empathetic communication, we can build stronger connections and collaborations across cultural boundaries. This approach promotes a deeper understanding of diverse perspectives and contributes to the development of ethically sound and culturally appropriate solutions.

7

Chapter 7: The Role of Empathy in Design Thinking

Design thinking, a human-centered approach to problem-solving, places empathy at the core of the innovation process. By deeply understanding the needs, desires, and pain points of users, innovators can create solutions that are not only effective but also compassionate and ethical. In this chapter, we will explore the role of empathy in design thinking, highlighting its potential to drive ethical innovation and create a positive impact on society.

Empathy involves immersing oneself in the user's experience, observing their behavior, and listening to their stories. This deep understanding allows innovators to identify unmet needs and uncover opportunities for creating meaningful solutions. By prioritizing empathy, we ensure that our innovations are grounded in the real-world experiences of users, leading to more effective and relevant outcomes.

One of the key techniques for fostering empathy in design thinking is user research. This involves conducting interviews, surveys, and observations to gather insights into users' lives. By engaging with users directly, we can gain a nuanced understanding of their challenges and aspirations. These insights serve as a foundation for the ideation and prototyping phases, guiding the development of solutions that truly resonate with users.

Another important aspect of empathy in design thinking is the creation of personas. Personas are fictional representations of target users, based on the insights gathered during user research. These personas help innovators maintain a user-centered focus throughout the design process, ensuring that the solutions are tailored to the specific needs and preferences of the target audience. By keeping personas in mind, we can create more inclusive and empathetic solutions that address the diverse experiences of users.

Empathy also plays a crucial role in the iterative nature of design thinking. By continuously seeking feedback from users and iterating on prototypes, we can refine our solutions to better meet their needs. This iterative process not only enhances the effectiveness of the innovation but also reinforces the ethical commitment to creating solutions that are truly user-centered. By embracing empathy, we can drive ethical innovation that positively impacts society.

8

Chapter 8: The Power of Collaboration

Collaboration, the act of working together towards a common goal, is a driving force behind ethical innovation. By pooling diverse perspectives, skills, and knowledge, we can create more holistic and inclusive solutions that address the complex challenges of our time. This chapter will examine the power of collaboration, showcasing how interdisciplinary partnerships and cross-cultural exchanges can lead to innovative breakthroughs that are both ethically sound and socially impactful.

At the heart of collaboration lies the principle of synergy—the idea that the collective effort of a group can achieve more than the sum of its individual parts. This synergy is particularly powerful in the realm of innovation, as it allows for the integration of diverse perspectives and expertise. By fostering a collaborative environment, we can leverage the unique strengths of each team member, leading to more comprehensive and well-rounded solutions.

One of the key benefits of collaboration is the ability to draw on a wide range of knowledge and skills. Interdisciplinary teams, composed of individuals with different backgrounds and areas of expertise, can approach problems from multiple angles. This diversity of thought leads to more creative and innovative solutions, as team members challenge each other's assumptions and contribute fresh perspectives. By embracing interdisciplinary collaboration, we can drive ethical innovation that is both innovative and effective.

Cross-cultural collaboration is another powerful driver of ethical innovation. By bringing together individuals from different cultural backgrounds, we can tap into a wealth of diverse experiences and viewpoints. This cultural diversity enriches the innovation process, ensuring that solutions are inclusive and respectful of different perspectives. By promoting cross-cultural exchanges, we can create a more equitable and just world, where innovative solutions are developed with a deep understanding of cultural contexts.

Collaboration also fosters a sense of shared ownership and accountability. When individuals work together towards a common goal, they are more likely to take collective responsibility for the outcomes of their efforts. This shared accountability promotes ethical decision-making, as team members are motivated to consider the broader implications of their actions. By cultivating a collaborative culture, we can ensure that our innovative endeavors are guided by ethical principles and a commitment to the greater good.

9

Chapter 9: Leadership in Ethical Innovation

Leadership plays a crucial role in steering the course of ethical innovation. Visionary leaders, who embody emotional intelligence and cultural sensitivity, can inspire and guide their teams towards creating solutions that uphold ethical principles. This chapter will delve into the qualities of effective leaders in the realm of innovation, highlighting the importance of ethical leadership in driving transformative change.

One of the key qualities of an effective leader in ethical innovation is emotional intelligence. Emotionally intelligent leaders are adept at recognizing and managing their own emotions, as well as understanding and empathizing with the emotions of others. This emotional awareness enables leaders to create a supportive and inclusive environment, where team members feel valued and motivated. By fostering emotional intelligence, leaders can drive ethical innovation by promoting collaboration, trust, and empathy within their teams.

Cultural sensitivity is another essential quality of effective leaders in ethical innovation. Leaders who are culturally sensitive are attuned to the diverse backgrounds and experiences of their team members and stakeholders. They actively seek to understand and respect different cultural perspectives, fostering an environment of inclusivity and respect. By prioritizing cultural sensitivity, leaders can ensure that innovative solutions are developed with a deep appreciation for the diverse fabric of humanity.

Ethical leaders also possess a strong commitment to integrity and accountability. They set high ethical standards for themselves and their teams, consistently demonstrating honesty, transparency, and fairness in their actions. This commitment to integrity inspires trust and confidence, both within the team and among external stakeholders. By embodying these values, ethical leaders can guide their teams towards creating innovative solutions that uphold ethical principles and contribute to the common good.

Visionary thinking is another critical quality of effective leaders in ethical innovation. Visionary leaders are able to see the bigger picture, envisioning the potential impact of their innovative efforts on society. They are driven by a sense of purpose and a commitment to making a positive difference in the world. By articulating a clear and inspiring vision, these leaders can rally their teams around a shared goal, motivating them to pursue ethical innovation with passion and determination.

10

Chapter 10: The Ethics of Technology

As technology continues to evolve at a rapid pace, ethical considerations must remain at the forefront of innovation. This chapter will explore the ethical implications of emerging technologies, such as artificial intelligence, biotechnology, and cybersecurity, and provide a framework for ensuring that these advancements are developed and deployed responsibly. By examining the intersection of technology and ethics, we can navigate the challenges and opportunities of the digital age with integrity and foresight.

Artificial intelligence (AI) is one of the most transformative technologies of our time, with the potential to revolutionize various aspects of society. However, the development and deployment of AI also raise significant ethical concerns. Issues such as bias in algorithms, privacy, and the impact on employment must be carefully considered to ensure that AI is developed in a way that respects human rights and promotes social justice. By prioritizing ethical considerations in AI development, we can harness its potential for positive impact while mitigating potential harms.

Biotechnology, with its advancements in genetic engineering, personalized medicine, and synthetic biology, holds great promise for improving human health and well-being. However, these innovations also raise ethical questions related to genetic privacy, equity in access to treatments, and the potential for unintended consequences. By establishing robust ethical frameworks and regulatory guidelines, we can ensure that biotechnological advancements are pursued responsibly, with a focus on promoting health and well-being for all.

Cybersecurity is another critical area where ethical considerations play a vital role. As our reliance on digital technologies grows, so does the need to protect sensitive information and ensure the security of digital infrastructures. Ethical considerations in cybersecurity include issues of privacy, data protection, and the responsible handling of cyber threats. By adopting ethical practices in cybersecurity, we can safeguard individuals' rights and maintain trust in digital systems.

The rapid pace of technological advancement also calls for ongoing ethical reflection and dialogue. As new technologies emerge, we must continuously reassess their ethical implications and adapt our frameworks accordingly. This proactive approach ensures that we remain vigilant in addressing potential ethical challenges and fostering responsible innovation. By prioritizing ethics in technology, we can navigate the digital age with integrity and a commitment to the greater good.

11

Chapter 11: Balancing Profit and Purpose

In the pursuit of innovation, balancing profit and purpose is a critical challenge that many organizations face. This chapter will explore strategies for aligning business goals with ethical values, ensuring that innovation efforts contribute to the greater good while achieving financial sustainability. By examining case studies of companies that have successfully navigated this balance, we can glean insights into how to create a more equitable and socially responsible business landscape.

One strategy for balancing profit and purpose is the adoption of a triple bottom line approach, which considers social, environmental, and financial performance. This holistic perspective encourages organizations to pursue sustainable practices that benefit society and the planet, while also achieving economic success. By integrating the triple bottom line into their business models, companies can create value for all stakeholders and contribute to long-term sustainability.

Corporate social responsibility (CSR) initiatives are another effective way for organizations to align profit with purpose. CSR involves voluntary actions that go beyond legal requirements to address social and environmental issues. These initiatives can take various forms, such as philanthropy, community engagement, and environmentally friendly practices. By incorporating CSR into their core strategies, companies can demonstrate their commitment to ethical innovation and build trust with stakeholders.

Impact investing is another powerful tool for balancing profit and purpose. This approach involves directing capital towards ventures that generate positive social and environmental outcomes, alongside financial returns. Impact investors prioritize projects that address pressing societal challenges, such as poverty, climate change, and healthcare access. By supporting these ventures, investors can drive ethical innovation and create meaningful change while achieving financial success.

Ethical leadership plays a crucial role in balancing profit and purpose. Leaders who prioritize ethical values and social responsibility can inspire their teams to pursue innovative solutions that align with the greater good. By fostering a culture of integrity and accountability, ethical leaders can guide their organizations towards achieving a harmonious balance between profit and purpose. This approach not only benefits society but also enhances the long-term success and reputation of the organization.

12

Chapter 12: Innovation in the Public Sector

The public sector, with its mandate to serve the common good, plays a pivotal role in driving ethical innovation. This chapter will examine the unique challenges and opportunities faced by government agencies and public institutions in fostering innovation that benefits society at large. By exploring examples of successful public sector innovations, we can identify best practices for creating policies and initiatives that promote ethical and inclusive progress.

One of the key challenges faced by the public sector is the need to balance innovation with accountability and transparency. Government agencies must ensure that their innovative efforts are aligned with public interest and subject to rigorous oversight. This requires the establishment of clear ethical guidelines and frameworks that govern the development and implementation of new solutions. By prioritizing accountability and transparency, the public sector can build trust with citizens and ensure that innovation serves the greater good.

Public-private partnerships (PPPs) are an effective strategy for driving innovation in the public sector. By collaborating with private enterprises, government agencies can leverage the expertise, resources, and agility of the private sector to develop innovative solutions to societal challenges.

These partnerships can take various forms, such as joint ventures, research collaborations, and infrastructure projects. By fostering PPPs, the public sector can enhance its capacity to drive ethical innovation and create positive social impact.

Citizen engagement is another crucial aspect of public sector innovation. By involving citizens in the decision-making process, government agencies can ensure that their innovative efforts are responsive to the needs and priorities of the community. This can be achieved through various means, such as participatory budgeting, public consultations, and digital platforms for citizen feedback. By promoting citizen engagement, the public sector can create more inclusive and democratic innovation processes.

Open data initiatives are also a powerful tool for fostering innovation in the public sector. By making data accessible to the public, government agencies can promote transparency, accountability, and collaboration. Open data enables citizens, researchers, and entrepreneurs to analyze and utilize information for various purposes, such as developing new services, improving public policies, and driving social change. By embracing open data, the public sector can create a fertile ground for ethical innovation and public trust.

13

Chapter 13: The Role of Education in Ethical Innovation

Education is a cornerstone of ethical innovation, as it equips individuals with the knowledge, skills, and values needed to navigate the complexities of the modern world. This chapter will explore the role of education in fostering a culture of ethical innovation, highlighting the importance of incorporating emotional intelligence, cultural sensitivity, and ethical principles into curricula. By examining innovative educational models, we can envision a future where ethical innovation is a fundamental aspect of learning.

One of the key components of ethical education is the development of emotional intelligence. By teaching students to recognize, understand, and manage their emotions, we can equip them with the skills needed to navigate complex social dynamics and make ethical decisions. Emotional intelligence education can be integrated into various subjects and activities, such as social-emotional learning programs, mindfulness practices, and collaborative projects. By prioritizing emotional intelligence, we can foster a generation of ethical innovators who are empathetic, compassionate, and socially responsible.

Cultural sensitivity is another essential aspect of ethical education. By exposing students to diverse cultures, perspectives, and experiences, we can promote an understanding and appreciation of cultural diversity. This can be achieved through various means, such as multicultural curricula, exchange programs, and inclusive teaching practices. By fostering cultural sensitivity, we can create an educational environment that values diversity and promotes ethical innovation that respects and embraces different cultural contexts.

Ethical principles should also be integrated into the educational curriculum. By teaching students about ethical theories, frameworks, and real-world applications, we can equip them with the tools needed to navigate complex ethical dilemmas. This can be achieved through various subjects, such as philosophy, ethics, and social studies, as well as through interdisciplinary approaches that incorporate ethical considerations into science, technology, engineering, and mathematics (STEM) education. By prioritizing ethical education, we can prepare students to become ethical innovators who are committed to creating positive social impact.

Innovative educational models, such as project-based learning and experiential learning, also play a crucial role in fostering ethical innovation. These models emphasize hands-on, real-world experiences that encourage students to apply their knowledge and skills to address real-world challenges. By engaging students in projects that promote social justice, environmental sustainability, and community well-being, we can inspire them to become ethical innovators who are driven by a sense of purpose and commitment to the greater good.

14

Chapter 14: The Impact of Globalization on Innovation

Globalization, the interconnectedness of our world, has a profound impact on the landscape of innovation. This chapter will examine how global trends and cross-cultural interactions influence the development of new solutions, highlighting the importance of cultural awareness and ethical considerations in a globalized context. By understanding the dynamics of globalization, we can create innovations that are not only impactful but also respectful of diverse cultural perspectives.

One of the key impacts of globalization on innovation is the increased flow of ideas, knowledge, and technology across borders. This global exchange fosters a rich and dynamic environment for innovation, as individuals and organizations can draw on a diverse array of perspectives and expertise. By embracing this diversity, we can create more inclusive and innovative solutions that address the complex challenges of our interconnected world.

Cross-cultural collaboration is another significant aspect of globalization that drives innovation. By bringing together individuals from different cultural backgrounds, we can tap into a wealth of diverse experiences and viewpoints. This cultural diversity enriches the innovation process, ensuring that solutions are inclusive and respectful of different perspectives. By promoting cross-cultural exchanges, we can create a more equitable and just world, where innovative solutions are developed with a deep understanding of cultural contexts.

Globalization also presents unique ethical challenges that must be navigated with care. Issues such as cultural appropriation, exploitation, and unequal access to resources can arise in the context of global innovation. By prioritizing ethical considerations and cultural sensitivity, we can ensure that our innovative efforts are respectful and inclusive of diverse cultural perspectives. This approach promotes a more equitable and just global innovation landscape.

The impact of globalization on innovation also calls for a commitment to sustainability and social responsibility. As we develop new solutions, we must consider their environmental and social implications, ensuring that they contribute to the well-being of our planet and its inhabitants. By adopting sustainable practices and prioritizing social responsibility, we can create innovations that drive positive change on a global scale.

15

Chapter 15: Ethical Considerations in Research and Development

Research and development (R&D) are the engines of innovation, driving the discovery and creation of new technologies, products, and services. This chapter will explore the ethical considerations that must guide R&D efforts, emphasizing the importance of transparency, accountability, and inclusivity. By examining best practices in ethical R&D, we can ensure that the innovations of tomorrow are developed with integrity and respect for all stakeholders.

Transparency is a foundational ethical principle in R&D, as it fosters trust and accountability among researchers, stakeholders, and the public. Transparent practices involve openly sharing information about research methodologies, data, and findings, allowing for independent verification and scrutiny. By prioritizing transparency, we can ensure that R&D efforts are conducted with integrity and that the resulting innovations are credible and trustworthy.

Accountability is another critical ethical consideration in R&D. Researchers and organizations must take responsibility for the potential impacts of their work, both positive and negative. This involves conducting thorough risk assessments, seeking input from diverse stakeholders, and implementing measures to mitigate potential harms. By embracing accountability, we can ensure that R&D efforts are aligned with ethical principles and contribute to the greater good.

Inclusivity is also essential in ethical R&D, as it ensures that diverse perspectives and experiences are considered throughout the research process. This involves actively engaging with underrepresented groups, fostering collaboration across disciplines, and creating opportunities for meaningful participation. By promoting inclusivity, we can create more equitable and innovative solutions that address the needs of diverse communities.

Ethical R&D also requires a commitment to ongoing reflection and improvement. As new technologies and methodologies emerge, researchers must continuously reassess the ethical implications of their work and adapt their practices accordingly. This proactive approach ensures that R&D efforts remain aligned with evolving ethical standards and societal values. By prioritizing ethical considerations in R&D, we can drive innovation that is responsible, inclusive, and beneficial for all.

16

Chapter 16: The Role of Media in Shaping Ethical Innovation

Media, as a powerful influence on public perception and opinion, plays a crucial role in shaping the landscape of ethical innovation. This chapter will explore how media can promote ethical innovation by raising awareness, highlighting best practices, and fostering informed dialogue. By examining the impact of media on innovation, we can identify strategies for leveraging its power to drive positive change and ethical progress.

One of the key ways media influences ethical innovation is through raising awareness of important issues and emerging trends. By reporting on groundbreaking research, technological advancements, and social challenges, media outlets can inform the public and spark conversations about the ethical implications of innovation. This awareness-building role helps to ensure that ethical considerations are part of the broader discourse on innovation.

Media also has the power to highlight best practices in ethical innovation, showcasing examples of organizations and individuals who are leading the way in responsible and inclusive innovation. These stories serve as valuable case studies, offering insights and inspiration for others to follow. By celebrating ethical innovation, media can create a positive feedback loop that encourages more organizations to adopt ethical practices and strive for excellence.

Informed dialogue is another crucial aspect of media's role in shaping ethical innovation. By providing a platform for diverse voices and perspectives, media outlets can facilitate meaningful discussions about the ethical challenges and opportunities presented by new technologies and solutions. This dialogue promotes a deeper understanding of complex issues and helps to build consensus on ethical standards and best practices. By fostering informed dialogue, media can contribute to a more thoughtful and nuanced approach to innovation.

The ethical responsibilities of media itself must also be considered. Media organizations have a duty to report accurately, fairly, and responsibly, avoiding sensationalism and bias. By upholding high ethical standards in their reporting, media outlets can build trust with their audiences and contribute to a more informed and ethically aware public. This commitment to ethical journalism is essential for shaping a landscape of ethical innovation that is grounded in truth and integrity.

17

Chapter 17: The Future of Ethical Innovation

As we look towards the future, the importance of ethical innovation becomes increasingly clear. This concluding chapter will envision the future of ethical innovation, exploring emerging trends, potential challenges, and opportunities for growth. By reflecting on the insights gained throughout this journey, we can chart a course towards a more just, equitable, and innovative world. Through the power of social dynamics and emotional intelligence, we can create a future where ethical innovation thrives, benefiting humanity as a whole.

One of the key trends shaping the future of ethical innovation is the growing emphasis on sustainability. As environmental concerns become more pressing, innovators are increasingly prioritizing sustainable practices and solutions that minimize harm to the planet. This shift towards sustainability is driving the development of green technologies, circular economy models, and eco-friendly products. By embracing sustainable innovation, we can create a future where technological progress goes hand in hand with environmental stewardship.

Another emerging trend is the integration of artificial intelligence (AI) and machine learning into various aspects of innovation. While AI holds great promise for enhancing efficiency, accuracy, and personalization, it also raises significant ethical considerations. Issues such as algorithmic bias, data privacy, and the impact on employment must be carefully addressed to ensure that AI is developed and deployed responsibly. By prioritizing ethical considerations in AI innovation, we can harness its potential for positive impact while mitigating potential risks.

The rise of social entrepreneurship is also shaping the future of ethical innovation. Social entrepreneurs are driven by a mission to address social and environmental challenges through innovative solutions that generate both social impact and financial returns. This approach is fostering the development of ventures that prioritize purpose alongside profit, creating a more inclusive and equitable business landscape. By supporting social entrepreneurship, we can drive ethical innovation that creates meaningful change in society.

The future of ethical innovation also calls for a commitment to continuous learning and adaptation. As new challenges and opportunities emerge, innovators must remain agile and open to evolving ethical standards and practices. This proactive approach ensures that innovation remains aligned with the values and needs of society. By fostering a culture of continuous improvement and ethical reflection, we can create a future where ethical innovation thrives, benefiting humanity as a whole.

Cultural Currents: How Social Dynamics and Emotional Intelligence Shape Ethical Innovation

In a world where the rapid pace of technological advancement constantly reshapes our lives, the need for ethical innovation has never been more pressing. "Cultural Currents" delves into the profound impact of social dynamics and emotional intelligence on the ethical landscape of innovation. This book offers a comprehensive exploration of how culture, social interactions, and emotional awareness shape the development of solutions that are not only groundbreaking but also grounded in ethical principles.

Spanning 17 insightful chapters, "Cultural Currents" takes readers on a journey through the intricate tapestry of culture, the dance of social dynamics, and the heartbeat of emotional intelligence. It highlights the synergy of these forces and their collective power to drive transformative, ethical innovation.

CHAPTER 17: THE FUTURE OF ETHICAL INNOVATION

With an emphasis on cultural sensitivity, empathy, and collaboration, this book provides practical strategies for creating inclusive, responsible, and impactful innovations that respect the diverse fabric of humanity.

From exploring ethical frameworks and the role of empathy in design thinking to examining the impact of globalization and the ethics of emerging technologies, "Cultural Currents" equips readers with the knowledge and tools needed to navigate the complexities of modern innovation. It emphasizes the importance of balancing profit and purpose, the unique role of the public sector, and the critical influence of media in shaping ethical innovation.

Ideal for innovators, leaders, educators, and anyone passionate about creating a better world, "Cultural Currents" offers a visionary blueprint for harnessing the power of social dynamics and emotional intelligence to drive ethical progress. By fostering a culture of continuous learning, reflection, and inclusivity, this book envisions a future where ethical innovation thrives, benefiting humanity as a whole.

www.ingramcontent.com/pod-product-compliance
Lightning Source LLC
LaVergne TN
LVHW010441070526
838199LV00066B/6122